# FRUITS YOU LOVE TO EAT
## ORANGES

AMY CULLIFORD

## A Crabtree Roots Book

Crabtree Publishing

crabtreebooks.com

# School-to-Home Support for Caregivers and Teachers

This book helps children grow by letting them practice reading. Here are a few guiding questions to help the reader with building his or her comprehension skills. Possible answers appear here in red.

## Before Reading:

• What do I think this book is about?
  • *I think this book is about how eating oranges is healthy.*
  • *I think this book will tell me that orange juice is made from oranges.*

• What do I want to learn about this topic?
  • *I want to learn why oranges taste so sweet.*
  • *I want to learn why oranges have peels.*

## During Reading:

• I wonder why...
  • *I wonder why oranges grow on trees while other fruits grow on plants.*
  • *I wonder why many orange trees have small white flowers.*

• What have I learned so far?
  • *I have learned that oranges are fruits.*
  • *I have learned that all orange trees have green leaves.*

## After Reading:

• What details did I learn about this topic?
  • *I have learned that oranges start off as little and green.*
  • *I have learned that over time oranges grow big and turn orange.*

• Read the book again and look for the vocabulary words.
  • *I see the word **flowers** on page 6 and the word **juice** on page 12. The other vocabulary words are found on page 14.*

**Oranges** are **fruits**.

All oranges come from orange **trees**.

Many orange trees have white **flowers**.

All orange trees
have green **leaves**.

Oranges grow from little and green to big and orange!

I like to make orange **juice** with oranges. Yum!

# Word List
## Sight Words

| | | |
|---|---|---|
| all | green | make |
| and | grow | many |
| are | have | to |
| big | I | white |
| come | like | with |
| from | little | |

## Words to Know

**flowers**

**fruits**

**juice**

**leaves**

**oranges**

**trees**

# 40 Words

**Oranges** are **fruits**.

All oranges come from orange **trees**.

Many orange trees have white **flowers**.

All orange trees have green **leaves**.

Oranges grow from little and green to big and orange!

I like to make orange **juice** with oranges. Yum!

# FRUITS YOU LOVE TO EAT
## ORANGES

Written by: Amy Culliford

Designed by: Rhea Wallace

Series Development: James Earley

Proofreader: Melissa Boyce

Educational Consultant: Marie Lemke M.Ed.

Photographs:
Shutterstock: Happy Author: cover; Posi Note: p. 3; alfredogarciatv: p. 5; Aoshi VN: p. 7; Steve Photography: p. 9; Andipapatonk: p. 11a; lunamarina: p. 11b; llike: p. 13

## Crabtree Publishing

crabtreebooks.com   800-387-7650
Copyright © 2024 Crabtree Publishing
All rights reserved. No part of this publication may be reproduced, stored in a retrieval system or be transmitted in any form or by any means, electronic, mechanical, photocopying, recording, or otherwise, without the prior written permission of Crabtree Publishing. In Canada: We acknowledge the financial support of the Government of Canada through the Canada Book Fund for our publishing activities.

Printed in Canada/122023/20231201

Published in Canada
Crabtree Publishing
616 Welland Ave.
St. Catharines, Ontario
L2M 5V6

Published in the United States
Crabtree Publishing
347 Fifth Ave
Suite 1402-145
New York, NY 10016

Library and Archives Canada Cataloguing in Publication
Available at Library and Archives Canada

Library of Congress Cataloging-in-Publication Data
Available at the Library of Congress

Hardcover: 978-1-0398-0975-8
Paperback: 978-1-0398-1028-0
Ebook (pdf): 978-1-0398-1134-8
Epub: 978-1-0398-1081-5